A FIRST LOOK BOOK

Earthquakes

David Lambert

Franklin Watts
London New York Toronto Sydney

First published in Great Britain
1982 by
Franklin Watts Ltd
12a Golden Square
London W1
Reprinted 1983

First published in the USA by
Franklin Watts Inc.
387 Park Avenue South
New York
N.Y. 10016

UK ISBN: 0 85166 956 5
US ISBN: 0-531-04372-X
Library of Congress Catalog Card
Number: 81-70050

Photographs supplied by
Colorific!
Popperfoto
Frank W. Lane
Science Museum
Space Frontiers Ltd

Illustrated by
Christopher Forsey
Hayward Art Group
Michael Roffe

Designed and produced by
David Jefferis

Technical consultant
John Salt BA, PhD

Printed in Great Britain by
Cambus Litho, East Kilbride

A FIRST LOOK BOOK

Earthquakes

Contents

Earthquake!

An earthquake is a violent shaking of the ground. It usually lasts for a minute or less. Yet no other natural event causes so much damage over so large an area in so short a time.

The side-effects can be terrible too – giant sea waves, landslides and avalanches have wrecked whole cities.

Even a mild quake is frightening. One eyewitness reports, "I woke up in bed to hear a shuddering, grinding sound. Everything was shaking and rattling. My bed shuffled across the hotel room, ending up jammed against the door. I was totally helpless."

Luckily, of the estimated million or so earthquakes which happen each year, less than a dozen are strong enough to cause loss of life.

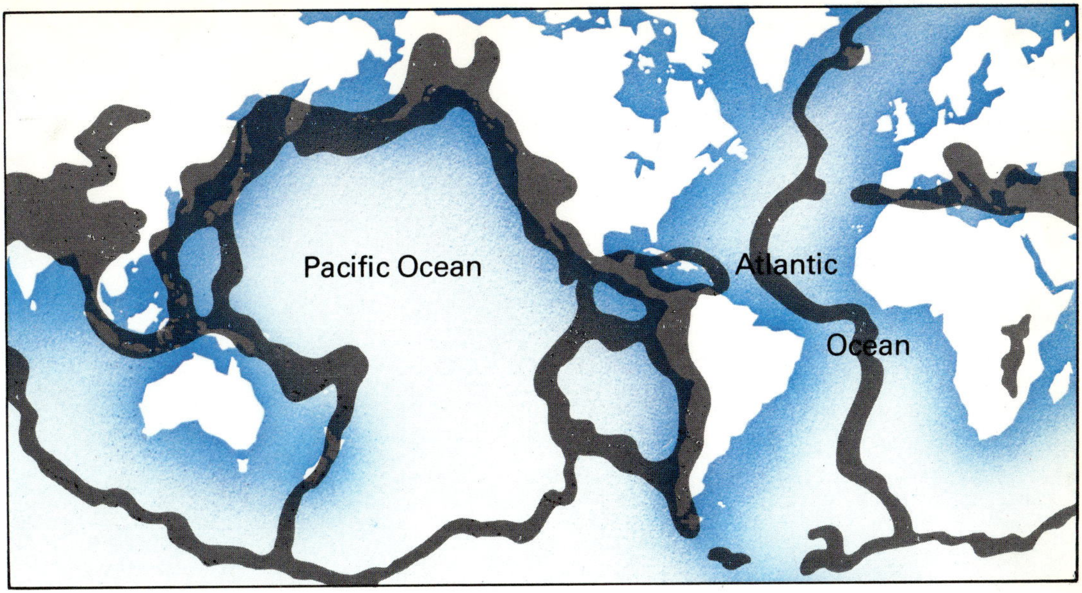

△ The grey areas on this map show where most earthquakes happen. More than three-quarters of all earthquake energy is released around the edges of the Pacific Ocean.

Cracks and faults

▽ These diagrams show an earthquake in action.
1 Stress builds up between two blocks of rock on either side of a tear fault.
2 The locked rocks bend with the strain.
3 The rocks snap past each other and back into shape again. The result is an earthquake.

Earthquakes happen where certain types of cracks occur in rock. Cracks run through most kinds of rock. In places, the rock on one side of a crack has moved against rock on the other side. The movement may be up, down or sideways. Where such a movement has taken place, the crack between the rocks is called a fault.

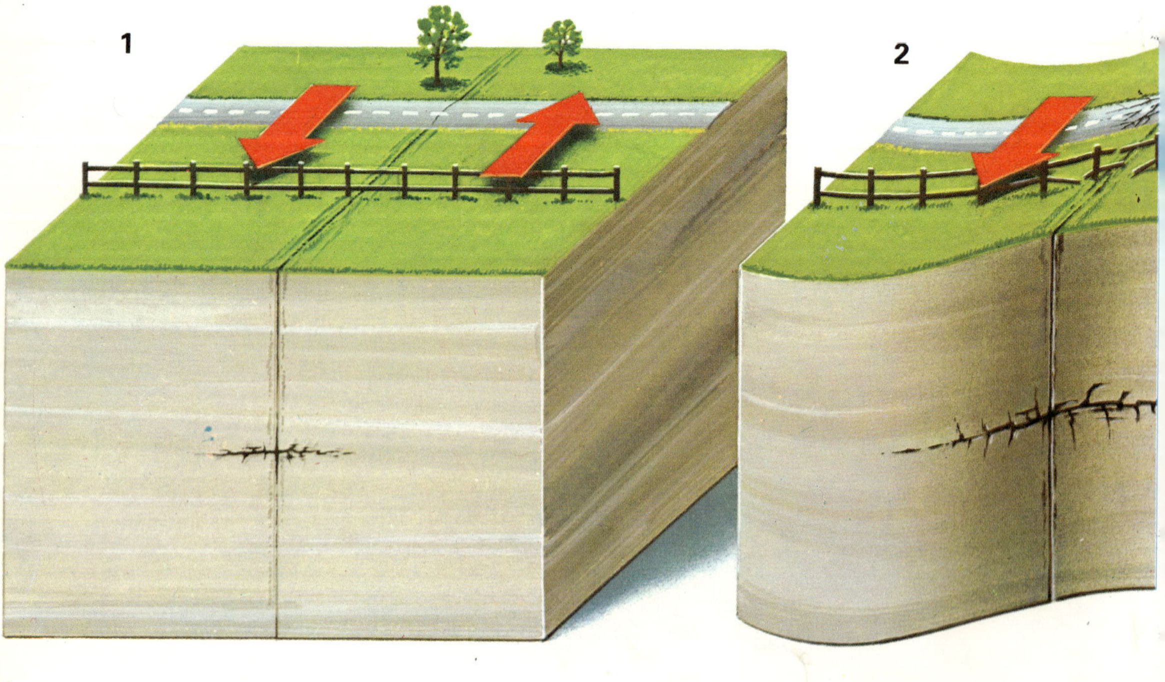

For years, the rock on one side of a fault may creep slowly past the other. Then both sides may jam together. Stress builds up inside the rocks until they start to bend.

At last the stress grows stronger than the bond which holds the blocks of rock together. The blocks move with a sudden jerk. The place where this happens is called the focus. From here vibrations speed out through the surrounding rocks as earthquake shocks. Smaller shocks may continue until the rocks have settled down.

△ Up-and-down movement caused these faults. On the left is a normal fault; on the right, a reverse fault, in which one block of rock is pushed up and over another.

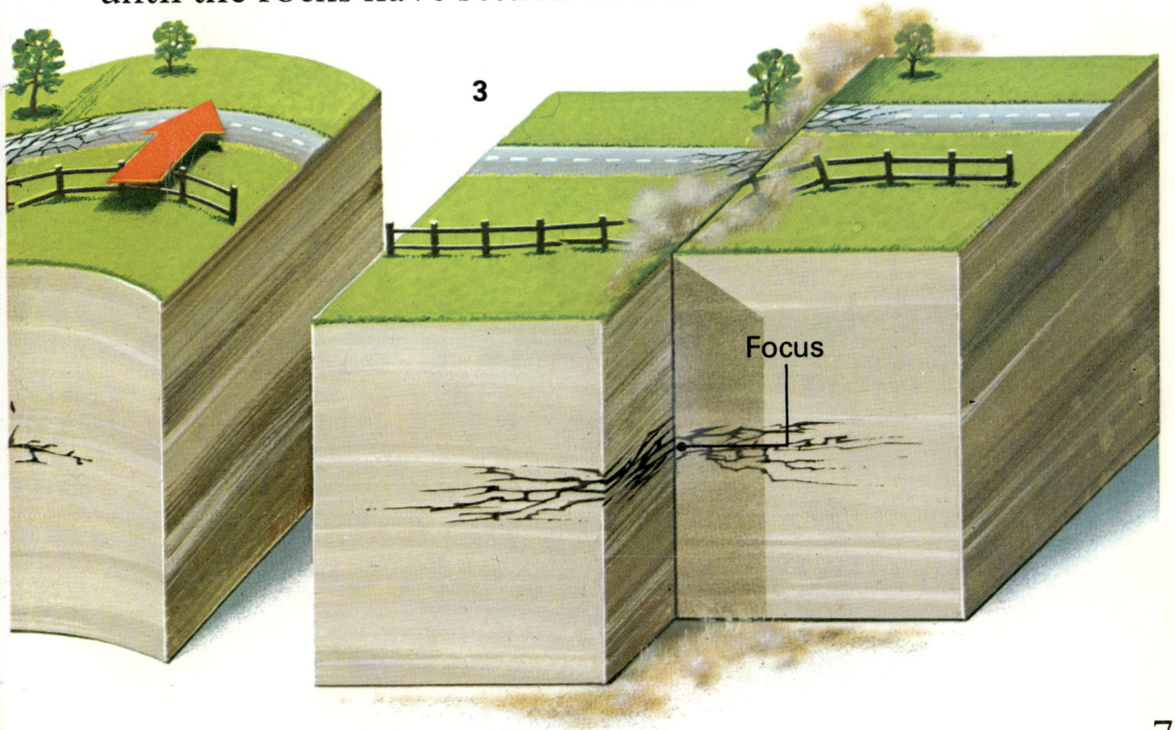

Changing the landscape

A fierce earthquake shock is over in just a minute or so, although weaker shocks may follow on and off for weeks. Yet that first, worst shock may leave the surface of the land completely changed.

In 1940 California's Imperial Valley earthquake shifted rows of orange trees aside. In 1967 an earthquake in Turkey raised a long, low mound across a field as if a giant mole had burrowed there.

Sometimes the change is much greater. In the San Francisco quake of 1906, ground to the west of the San Andreas Fault moved northwards as much as 6 m (20 ft) for 430 km (267 miles). In Alaska in 1899 rocks from beneath the sea rose 14 m (47 ft) with barnacles still clinging to them. In 1923 parts of the floor of Japan's Sagami Bay dropped 300 m (1,000 ft), and the land around the bay swung clockwise.

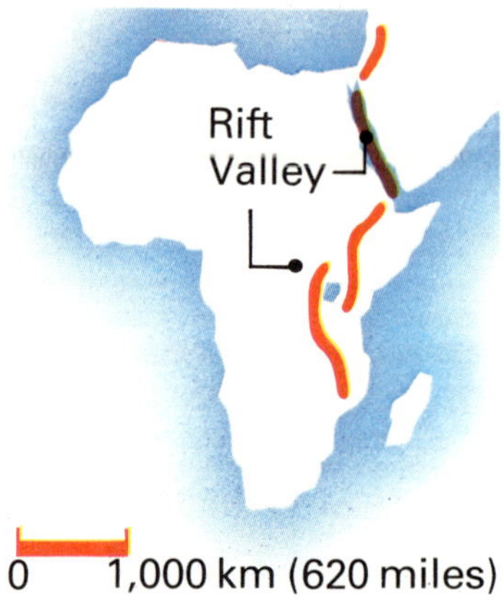

△ East Africa's Great Rift Valley, part of a huge fault system that runs for 6,400 km (4,000 miles).

On the right is a satellite photograph of the West Coast of America. An earthquake on the San Andreas Fault (arrowed) smashed San Francisco in 1906. Earthquakes often happen in the same places. It is possible that another quake may happen here.

Continents adrift

What makes an earthquake happen? The answer lies deep below the Earth's crust, the outer layer of hard rock that we live on.

The crust floats on the mantle, a thick layer of very hot, heavy rock hundreds of kilometres deep. Slow currents of sticky, molten rock flow up and around in the mantle. Where they hit the crust above, they spread out and can crack open the crust.

These movements have split the crust into giant jigsaw pieces known as crustal plates. The globes on the right show how at one time there was just one huge land mass. Now there are several. The continents we live on are each a part of one of these giant drifting plates.

As the plates move, their edges often meet in slow, grinding collisions. It is these collisions that are the main cause of earthquakes.

The world about 200 million years ago. All the continents were linked in one huge land mass, *Pangaea*.

△ The Earth's crust is split into huge crustal plates, which drift slowly across the world. Earthquake zones are at or near the edges of these plates.

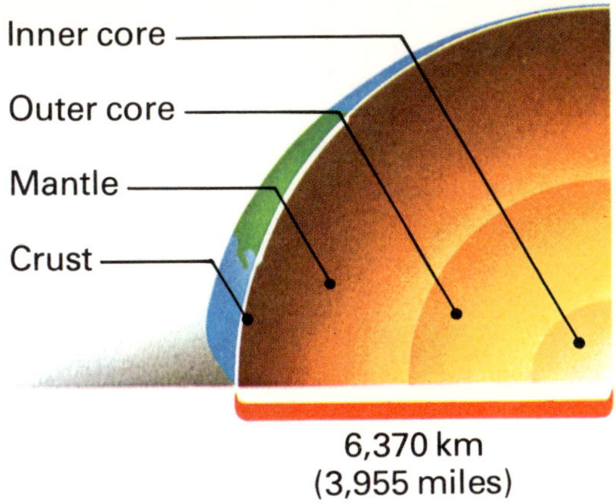

◁ This slice through the Earth shows the various layers within our planet. "Shallow-focus" earthquakes are the most common, starting no deeper than 70 km (44 miles). It is not known what causes earthquakes as far down as 700 km (450 miles).

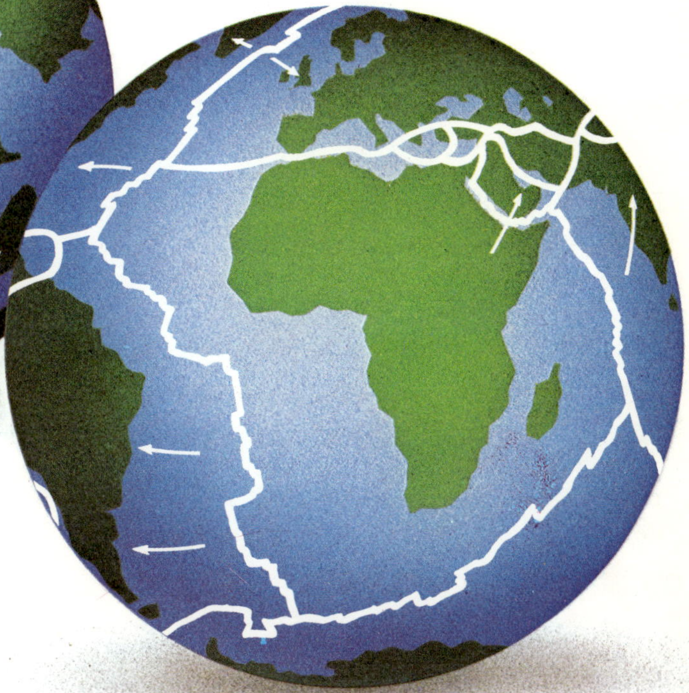

The world today, with the edges of the plates shown in white. Compare them with the earthquake zones map on page 5.

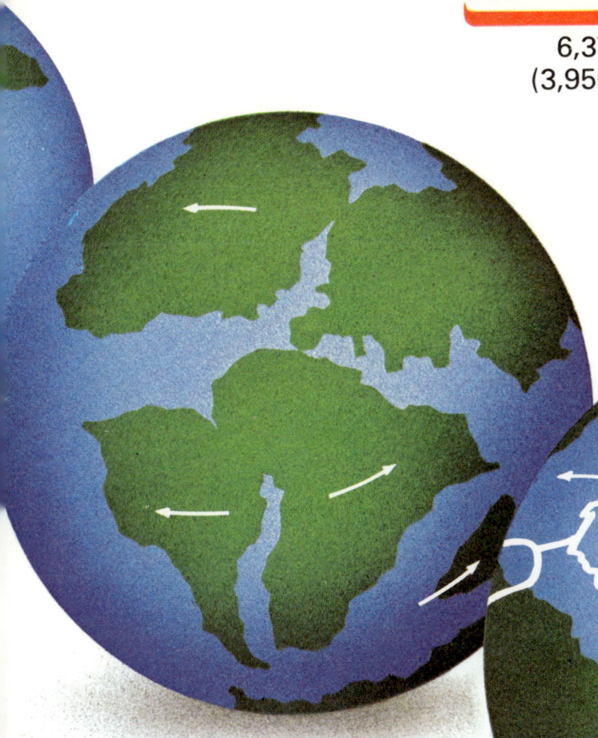

Pangaea gradually split into smaller land masses.

Underwater earthquakes

Many earthquakes occur beneath the sea. Their vibrations may cause giant sea waves called *tsunami*, a Japanese word meaning "storm wave".

Tsunamis travel far and fast. They can move across the Pacific Ocean at speeds of around 750 km/h (466 mph).

Out at sea, the waves may be hundreds of kilometres from crest to crest and only a metre or two high. But when they run up a sloping shore close to land, they pile up into towering waves 12 m (40 ft) or more high.

▽ This slice through the earth shows regions (1, 2, 3) where stresses in the rocks are likely to result in earthquakes.

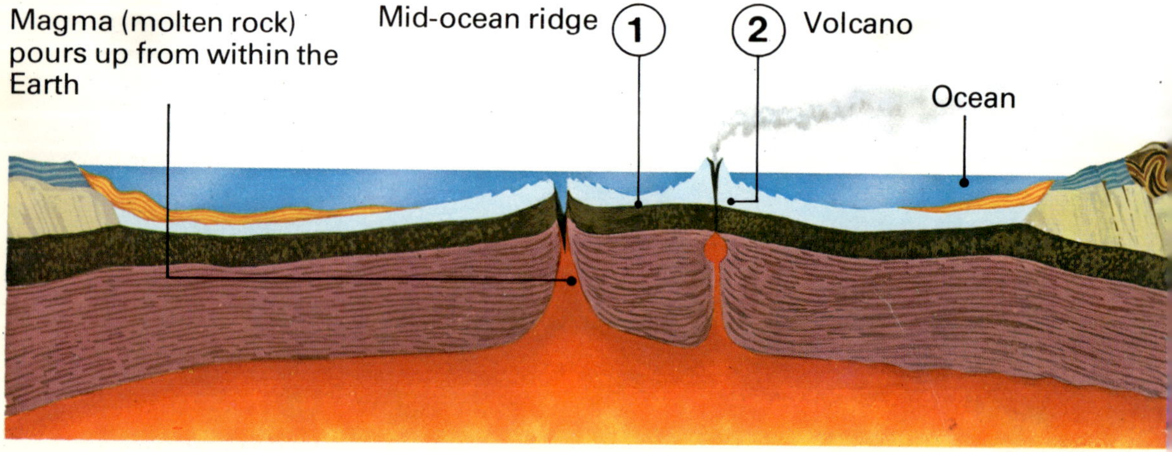

△ These cars were thrown together by the force of a tsunami which hit Hawaii in 1960. The waves had rolled all the way from Chile, over 9,500 km (6,000 miles) away.

Such waves can be deadly. Tsunamis that hit Japan in 1896 destroyed 11,000 homes and buildings and drowned 27,000 people.

Most tsunamis start on the rim of the Pacific Ocean. Islands like Hawaii have warning stations to mark their approach.

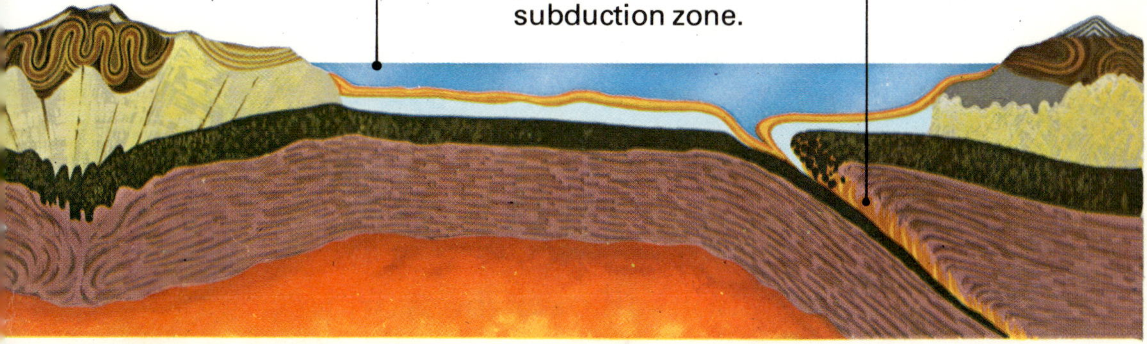

Seismographs

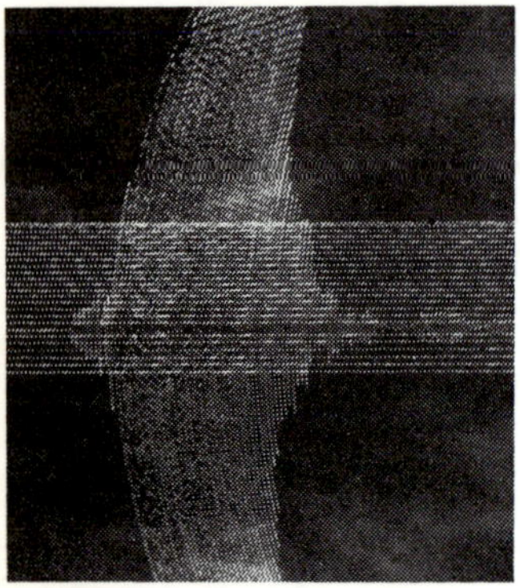

△ This seismograph trace was made in London in 1979. The cause was an earthquake in Yugoslavia, which measured 7 on the Richter scale. Over 120 people were killed and 10,000 were left homeless. Many people were injured and tidal waves caused further damage on the coast.

More than 1700 years ago a Chinese inventor made an unusual jar. Jutting from its sides were dragon's heads, each with a ball held in its jaws. If an earthquake shook the jar, the jaws opened and the balls fell into the gaping mouths of toy frogs sitting on the ground below. This was the first seismograph.

Seismographs are instruments that measure earthquake shocks. Very sensitive seismographs can magnify the trembling of the ground a million times. Different seismographs measure the strength of different kinds of earthquake wave moving through the ground. One type measures waves at least 800 km (500 miles) long.

Seismographs help scientists to measure the strength of any earthquake and find its focus underground. There are hundreds of earthquake measuring stations all over the world.

By timing the earthquake waves, measuring stations can find out how far away the quake is. The measurements from three different stations are used to draw three circles. The point where they cross is directly above the earthquake focus. This is called the epicentre.

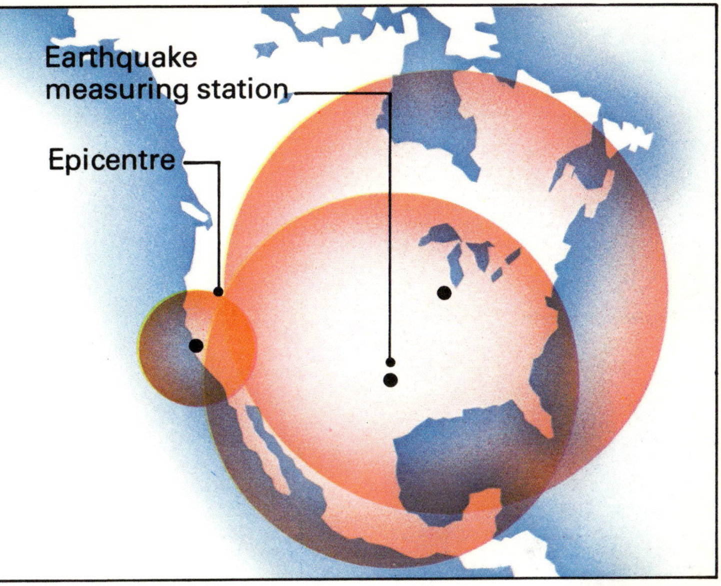

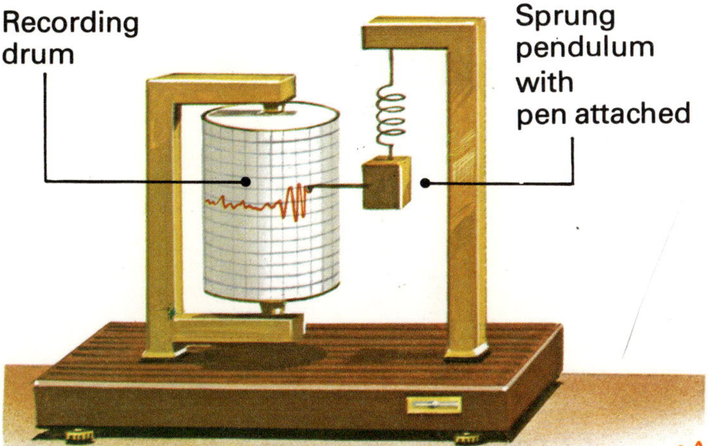

◁ The frame and drum of a seismograph shake with the earthquake shock. The pen, which is attached to a spring, remains still. The result is a wiggly line showing the force of the earthquake.

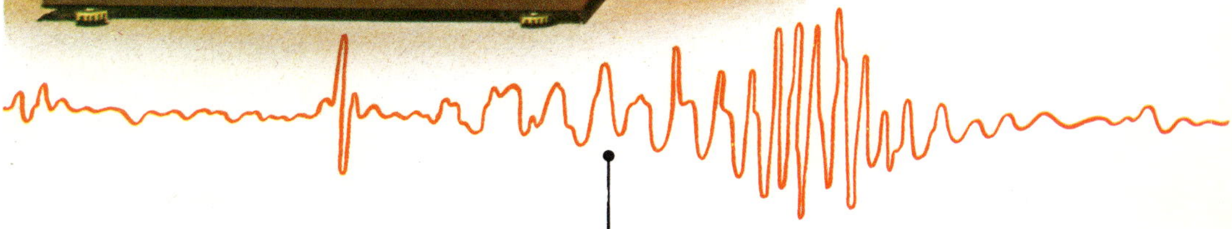

Measuring earthquakes

There are two ways of measuring an earthquake – the Richter scale and the Mercalli scale.

The Richter scale uses seismographs to measure the amount of energy released. Magnitude 2 on the scale is barely noticeable, while magnitude 8 will flatten a city.

The Mercalli scale, shown below, describes the actual damage caused by the earthquake.

▽ The diagram below shows the Mercalli scale, which indicates the "felt intensity" of earthquake shocks. It is not precise like the Richter scale, but it describes the sort of damage that people actually see and feel during an earthquake.

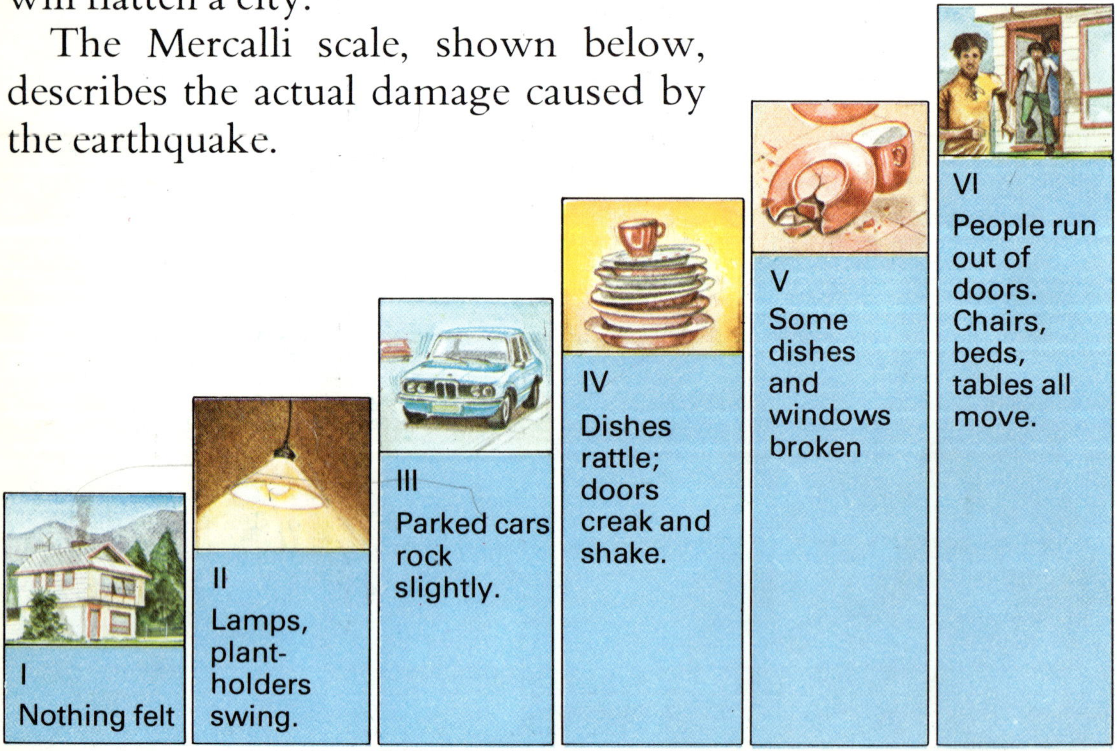

VII

Some chimneys broken

VIII

Some walls collapse. Statues and monuments fall over.

IX

Ground cracks. Well-designed buildings thrown out of line.

X

Rail lines bent. Landslides on slopes.

XI

Bridges destroyed. Few brick structures left standing. Broad fissures in ground.

XII

Ground heaves in waves. Objects thrown through the air. Damage total.

World's worst earthquakes

△ The wrecked City Hall of San Francisco after an earthquake devastated the city in 1906. The quake measured 8.3 on the Richter scale. Fires burned for days and over 500 people died.

The world's worst earthquakes have been severe shocks that hit crowded cities with buildings unable to stand up to violent shaking. These earthquakes are usually shallow, with a focus no more than 60 km (37 miles) below the ground.

East Asia has suffered most. An earthquake that hit China in 1556 may have killed 800,000 people – more than any earthquake since. No other earthquake destroyed more property than the shock that struck Yokohama and Tokyo in Japan in 1923.

Each year 1,000 earthquakes are strong enough to damage, yet only 10 or so kill many people. This is partly because some of the strongest earthquakes happen in places where few people live. For example, only 114 died in the Alaskan earthquake of 1964, although it was one of the strongest ever measured.

△ Anchorage, Alaska, after the earthquake of 1964. It holds the record as the longest-lasting earthquake ever. Forty seconds of gentle rolling motion were followed by four minutes of hard shaking. The main quake stopped after seven minutes, but aftershocks went on for nine months.

Some famous earthquakes

Year	Place	Damage
856	Corinth, Greece	45,000 killed
1556	Shensi, China	800,000 killed
1737	Calcutta, India	300,000 killed
1755	Lisbon, Portugal	60,000 killed
1906	San Francisco, USA	City burnt down
1908	Messina, Sicily	85,000 killed
1923	Kwanto Plain, Japan	143,000 killed. 576,000 dwellings destroyed
1939	Northern Turkey	100,000 casualties
1964	Alaska, USA	Damage cost $750 million
1966	Tashkent, USSR	200,000 homeless
1976	T'ang-shan, China	750,000 killed

Predicting earthquakes

△ Satellites may be useful for earthquake prediction. LAGEOS, shown here as a line across the sky in this time-exposure picture, uses a laser to measure the movements of the Pacific and North American plates. It should be able to show pre-shock movements.

In 1975 an earthquake smashed the Chinese city of Haicheng. Yet its citizens were safely camping in the countryside around. They had left their homes, warned of danger by the strange antics of animals such as dogs, pigs, rats and snakes. The animals' keen senses had told them of vibrations and gases escaping from the ground before people noticed anything amiss.

Nowadays scientists are discovering more clues that warn of coming earthquakes. Special instruments are being used in California, New Zealand and Japan to show whether strain is building up along a fault. Other instruments can detect a build-up of the gas radon in water underground, a sign of an earthquake to come.

Perhaps one day scientists will be able to reliably predict where and when the next big quake will happen in the world's earthquake zones.

Many scientists now think that strange animal behaviour before a quake is not coincidence. Pigeons have nerves in their legs which can detect faint vibrations. Dogs pick up faint smells and high-pitched sounds. Hammerhead sharks are aware of changes in electrical fields, while snakes detect faint smells too. All these may be clear signs of quakes to come.

Rescue!

A severe earthquake can destroy the homes of thousands and leave many people injured. It can also wreck water and electricity supplies. If roads and railways are destroyed, earthquake victims may be cut off from all help for days. Hunger, foul drinking water, and cold may endanger the survivors. Often all this happens in countries too poor to organize much aid.

Luckily, the Red Cross and other international relief organizations can bring help fast. They fly in doctors, nurses, medicines, material for setting broken limbs, tents, food, and water-purifying equipment.

However, helpers in a hurry sometimes make mistakes. In 1976 well-wishers sent over 100 tons of useless medicines to earthquake-shattered Guatemala, some of which dated from 1934. Emergency teams were unable to sort them out.

▷ Hercules transport planes fly in much-needed supplies to an earthquake-smashed area. Planes like this are useful as they can land and take off in very little space.

Under the tail of the nearest plane, crewmen and official discuss how best to get Red Cross aid to the survivors.

In the background, a mobile hospital has been flown in and is now set up to take care of the badly injured.

CF
1508

Earthquake protection

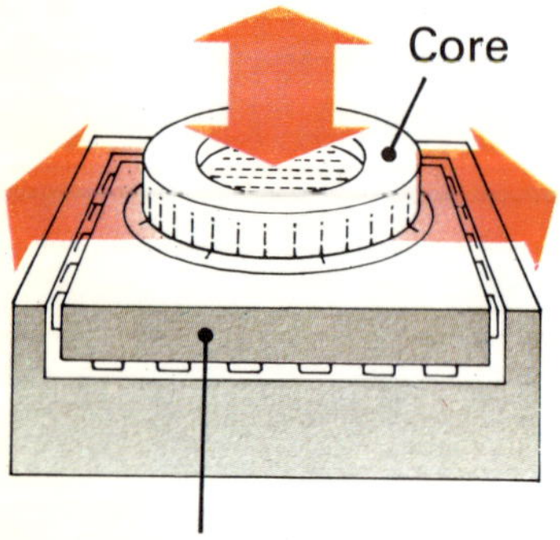

△ This picture shows the core of a nuclear power station being tested on a shaking table. If the designers have done their work right, the core will not crack and the power station should be safe to operate in an earthquake area.

In 1923 Tokyo's Imperial Hotel stood firm while buildings all around were falling down. Its architect, Frank Lloyd Wright, had designed its floor like a giant tray supported by a waiter's fingers. This enabled the hotel to absorb even the worst of the earthquake shocks.

Nearly all damage and loss of life is caused by collapsing buildings. Gas pipes and power cables snap. Sparks ignite the leaking gas and fires break out. People are buried under the wreckage or badly burned. Proper building design can prevent most of these casualties.

Architects now know of several ways of making buildings safe. If possible they build on solid rock, and not on soft clay, sand or gravel. In big buildings, they use reinforced concrete or a steel frame. If the ground shakes, the frame will hold the building firm.

◁ San Francisco's pyramid-shaped TransAmerica building was designed to be completely earthquake-proof.

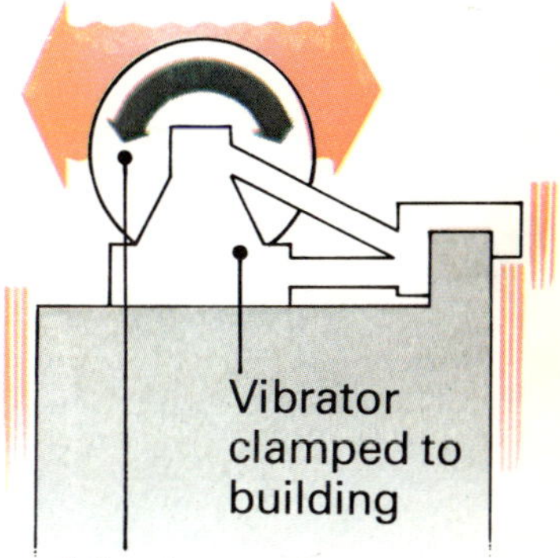

△ This odd-looking machine can be attached to the structure of a building. It causes the building to vibrate to see if it will stand up to earthquake shocks.

Prevention

In the early 1960s American soldiers in Colorado dug a well 3.5 km (2 miles) deep to get rid of waste material. Then they poured water containing the waste down the well. Unknown to the troops the water "oiled" a fault below the nearby city of Denver. One side of the fault had caught against the other. It gave way with a sudden jerk. The result was Denver's first earthquake for 80 years. The small shocks continued until the soldiers stopped pouring the waste.

This showed scientists that people could trigger tiny earthquakes. Therefore why not pour water down cracks like the San Andreas Fault? It might cause tiny quakes, but these should stop great strains building up underground and *prevent* a far bigger one happening later on.

Such schemes may one day quieten land that suffers savage tremors.

▷ This picture shows how a fault line could be "greased" by pumping down water. If the fault line is lubricated, the rocks can slide by each other in a series of small tremors rather than a single devastating earthquake.

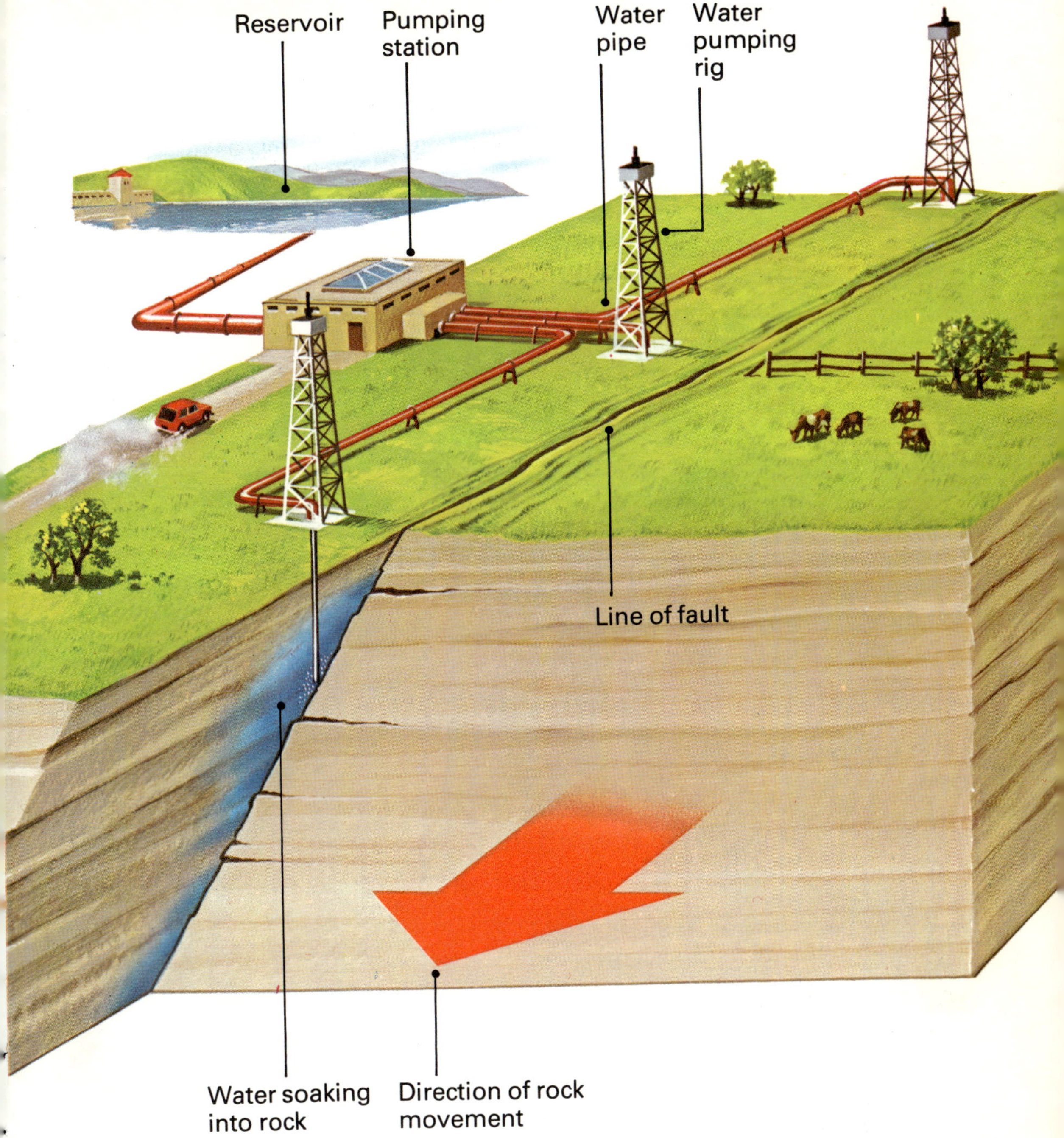
Reservoir
Pumping station
Water pipe
Water pumping rig
Line of fault
Water soaking into rock
Direction of rock movement

Using earthquakes

△ This explosion was set off under the seabed by geologists searching for oil. By analysing the quake waves, they can discover whether or not the rock formations contain oil or gas.

Earthquakes do more than just cause damage. They help scientists learn about the inside of the Earth.

This knowledge comes from studying the three main kinds of shock wave given off by earthquakes. P-waves (push waves) can travel right through the middle of the Earth. S-waves (shake waves) cannot pass through the Earth's core. L-waves (long-waves) only travel through the Earth's outer crust. The different speeds of these waves showed scientists that the Earth is made up of layers of different kinds of rock.

Geologists sometimes set off explosions in the ground and study the shock waves that bounce back. Such artificial earthquakes help them to discover useful kinds of rock inside Earth's outer crust. This is one way of finding likely places to drill for oil or mine for coal or minerals.

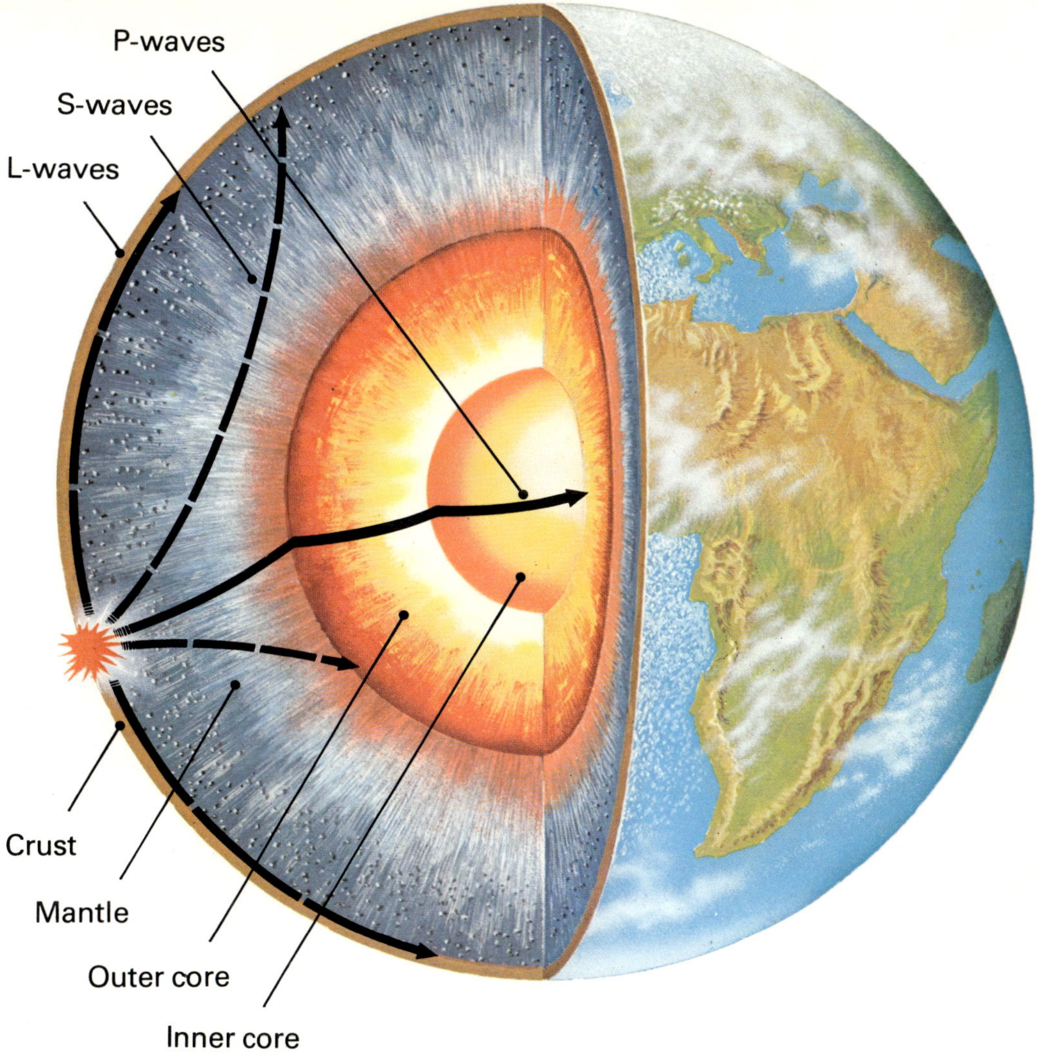

△ The three types of earthquake wave move at different speeds through the Earth. P-waves are the fastest, moving at 8–13 km/second (5–8 miles/second). S-waves travel at about half this, while L-waves dawdle along at just 3–5 km/second (2–3 miles/second). They follow curving paths through the various thicknesses of rock.

Glossary

Here are explanations of some of the technical words used in this book

Core
The centre of the Earth. Intensely hot, it is thought to be made of a liquid layer and an inner solid mass of iron and nickel.

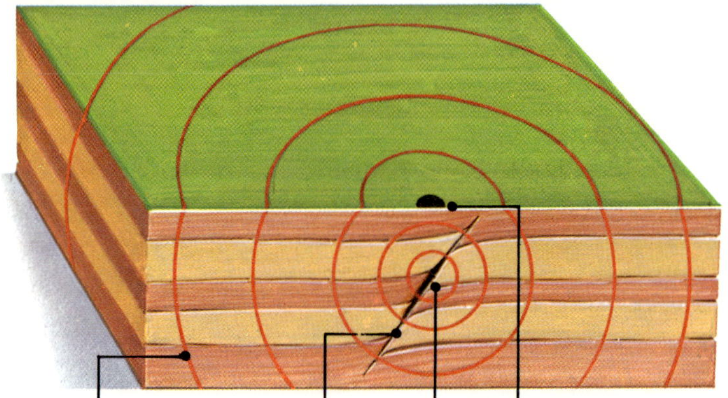

Crust
The Earth's rocky outer skin. It varies in depth from 40 km (25 miles) to 5 km (3 miles) under the seabed.

Crustal plate
A great slab of the Earth's crust. The biggest plates carry continents (such as Antarctica, Europe and so on) on top.

Epicentre
The ground surface directly above the focus of an earthquake.

Fault
A crack in the Earth's crust where rocks on either side move against each other, up, down or sideways. In a tear fault, the movement is sideways. In normal and thrust faults, movement is up or down.

Focus
The underground centre of an earthquake. This is usually less than 40 km (25 miles) deep. The deepest known focus was 720 km (447 miles) down.

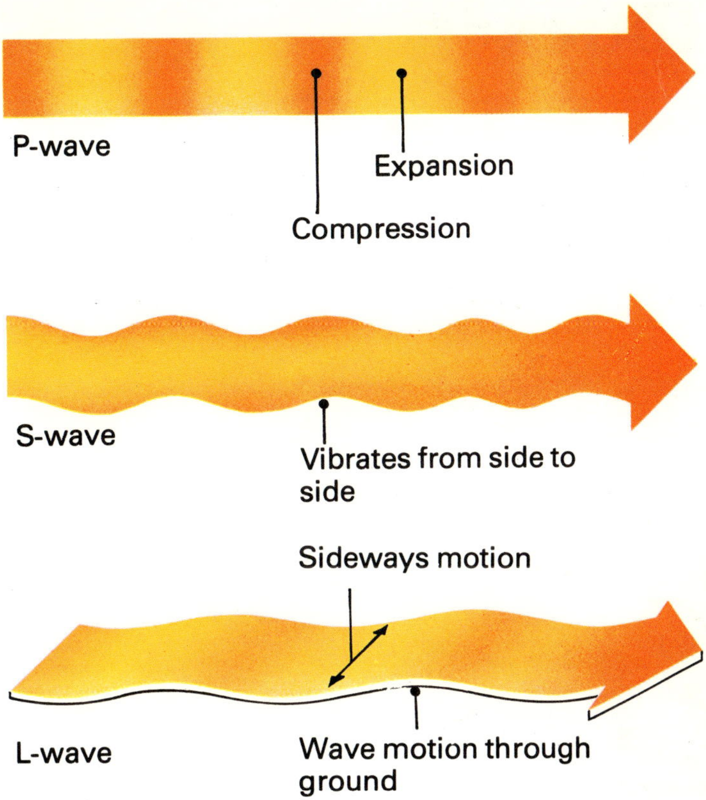

Mantle
The layer of hot rock immediately below the crust. Parts of the mantle are soft and flow like hot tar. The mantle is hundreds of kilometres deep.

Mercalli scale
A scale for measuring the felt intensity of an earthquake – its effects in any particular place.

Mid-ocean ridge
An underwater mountain ridge along the middle of an ocean. It is built of molten rock that rose through the widening gap between two crustal plates. On either side of the ridge are transform faults where underwater earthquakes usually happen.

Richter scale
Scale for measuring an earthquake's magnitude – the amount of energy it releases.

Rift Valley
A valley formed where land has sunk between two parallel faults.

Seismic wave
A wave of energy produced by an earthquake. There are three main kinds:
L-waves travel through the Earth's crust. They are really two waves in one; a side-to-side movement and an up-and-down rolling motion.
P-waves travel right through the Earth. They vibrate the rock backwards and forwards like a coiled spring.
S-waves pass through the crust and mantle but not the core. They cause the rock to vibrate from side to side like a guitar string.

Seismograph
An instrument for measuring earthquake shocks.

Subduction zone
A place where the edge of one plate is pushed down under the edge of another.

Index